Species of Spaces

Ken Bolton

Species of Spaces

Shearsman Books

First published in the United Kingdom in 2018 by
Shearsman Books
50 Westons Hill Drive
Emersons Green
Bristol BS16 7DF

Shearsman Books Ltd Registered Office
30–31 St. James Place, Mangotsfield, Bristol BS16 9JB
(this address not for correspondence)

www.shearsman.com

ISBN 978-1-84861-576-2

ACKNOWLEDGEMENTS
Friends Pam Brown, Laurie Duggan and Tim Wright have given advice—
that I have clearly not always taken—as well as encouragement (that many
will feel to have been contra-indicated). My thanks to these poets.

Some of these poems have been published in magazines
& anthologies before. Many thanks to their editors.
'Dark Heart' appeared in *Cordite* and *Best Australian Poems 2016*
'Hard Pressed', '(Spot Check)' and 'Polski Ogorki' in *Journal of Poetics
Research*; 'Gilbert Place' and 'What Do I Owe Them?' in *Australian Book
Review*; 'Tale Of Two Cities' in *Golden Handcuffs Review*.

Contents

1

In the Moment

In Three Parts:
A Report on the Ongoing Moment

1: Report

We fly out
a few hours late

after a security delay,
that makes the wait
more an adventure

— anxiously perilous —

an enormous
press of people

—all bets off,
all planes
delayed

the whole airport
ordered, again,
thru security —

less pissed off
than normally

& separated —
because we
booked our flights
separately.

I don't know
where Cath is sitting
or what she's doing—

well, reading probably
                    I've read
                    the first few

    of Kurt's artist's books

                the young-sounding one
                    FOR KATE
                        &
                    I HAVE
                NEVER BEEN TO JAPAN

lighter
        less sentimental, cannier,

                                & the suddenly serious
& existential one
on personality,
            WE ARE A MOVIE —
funny, but dark,
adult suddenly

            And I'm thinking now,
calibrating 'how it went'
                    the show

that brought us
all together

    (again)
& yet
hardly brought me together
with anyone.
     But it did:

       with Kurt, whom I've never
       been closer to, & Denis—

       & Laurie (whom
       I finally got to
       relax with—

on the train away, back to Sydney)

         The readings
were not, at least, divisive
       tho they probably made
          everybody
too nervous to relate much

       And we all went
for coffee
when the last was done.

I didn't get
to speak much
to Pam—to Micky
just a little,

  #

& Sal was gone.
      #

Steve never showed.

I hope
he's alright.

And the books got done

        —Kurt's hard work—

that I suppose
the others are
reading now, evaluating.

Are knives coming out?
Probably not.

        I had the best time
in the run-up, with Kurt

        we laughed & joked

& 'dealt with the gallery'
        'dealt with' the media

        — readied
        (steadied) —

& planned

    Then afterwards

cooking, serving up, drinking & laughing,
        with Denis,

Arnie, Laurie
& Cath —

#

the mellow team.

#

Arnie rolled
a big spliff.

The plan:
to sell Nick
a list
  of who had purchased
  the rare editions

   & a list
  'for him alone'—
    of who else
    had been given that list —

  Phew!

   We laugh about
Tranter
  going off for a drink, looking
     to see what's in the
      fridge
while the computer composes poems for him
    —the Terminals—

sipping a daiquiri
& watching the pool-cleaner
smuggle slowly back & forth

I imagine a large
tadpole-looking shape,

going slowly,
from one end

to the other,

black against the
pale blue of the tiles.

(I've never seen
a pool-cleaner in fact.)

The Erudition model,
manufactured by Clepsydra.

#

And the Bard
from the Bush:

pretending to be
dumber than he is,

an innocent—

wise-foolin'.

— 'Wise Foolin' —

(to the tune of
'Barefootin')

When will he
drop off the peg?

    #

Laurie thinks his
own real work began
around that time,
           '79, 80

Tho there are continuities
running right back —

& to *Under The Weather*,
at least —
           tho his language

became more spare
from the 80s on

                     & there is a
                     sureness
no equivocation
in the face
of others' doubts
            (if not his own)

Pam's work
changed then, too,
& continued to change,

15

And then there's mine
— my abiding problem.

When does this plane land?

2: What Is to Be Done?

I have become couth mainly by aping my friends

True?

> #

I write to Johnny J
                 tell him about Shearsman
our plans for The Poems

girls go by
                 —this University (so called)
is an *art* school—
                      in their new
winter clothes
              so they suddenly look more
                        'purposeful'
—than last week
                when it was all shorts
& t-shirts
            & a lot of off-the-shoulder.

About now the first assignments kick in.
They come in the shop looking determined
                   or puzzled
or desperate.
               I marshal my couth &
help —
          suggest 'the relevant texts'.

I think of sending Ron Padgett a postcard.

Should I?

#

Or a fan letter
I owe him one.

#

"John," I say,
To return to the problem —
'the poems'
(so called — ha ha)
<u>are</u> <u>looking</u> 'good' (! ?)

#

'bad' (?)

#

'indifferent' (?)

#

— what *do* I say?   In fact,
they *are* okay.
We wrote them one
afternoon
a week or so back

one every fifteen minutes
on average   & laughed a lot

(Do we always
'have

the stopwatch out'?
Non.)

amazed how
fast they were going.
Now to fix them.
Tinker, tinker.
John, pass that spanner!

Thirteen,
so we're calling them that,
subtitled
"Lucky for some".
They say that, John says, *at Bingo*

("One Three—Thirteen: lucky for some.")

'The Poems'

a phrase which always rings the Ted Berrigan bell
& says
The mania of the young poet
Have I put it behind me?
yet?
'really'?
(or)

                           Am I
                    THE VERY SPIRIT
                                   of Ted (!) ?

When it comes right down to it, any of those *'the-very-*
X-of ...'s
                 always amuse
                                  the spectacle of all those beliefs
I've never held—
                    so French, so ideal, so *German,* so Ted?
But Ted ist Tod, no?
                          (what language am I talking here?)

"John," I write,
                 "Here is what I've done." In response
to a letter of more or less the same from him.

That takes care of *those* poems,   for a few days.

                                   At work
an email from Pam, an email from Laurie.
                                   My world
closing in

                  reassuringly.

                              #

                     An afternoon,
                               then home

*

shopping on the way

*

(rain)

*

TV

*

The Poems

3: The Baby—The Bathwater

This morning—a baby at the gym.

                    "A tall one," says his mother
                          of her son
                          (Her own father was 6' 2")
Swedish.

         He'll be *paid* more, I say
                    Some statistic makes that claim
"I'll have to talk to my boss!" she says.   She herself is 5'11",
blonde. She places the baby close to her—
                         & does her weights
& moves
         smiling at him. A few words. He looks on,
                        looks at me
small, serious face

             #

Rae's email this morning
                with a funny
             poem-for-his-daughter
we discuss daughters
            his poem mentions Woodrow Wilson
so I figure, correctly,
            she's doing   International Studies
(the League of Nations
            the failure of liberalism
                         victory

of the Realists

        — so called —

                      I'm right, he says.

    #

Sushi for lunch

      #

              I ask what "Inari pack" means
as I've been eating it for years

                  Sushi, she says

or Cold Food or Tofu

            so I still don't know—

I don't care for any of the answers —

                so I'm happy to
                    return

to my base position

          (general ignorance)

                  I like them tho.

So much trouble at the bank

              I've had to forge the cheque,
              anyway —

as Julie had made a mistake

         (— & *it's her day off*)

But it turns out there are more errors even than the
                  bank noticed,

I agree to fill out an initialled change—

                              making it

my full signature.

                  (Julie's —forged— initials

                            have to stand.)

              #

I could boldly have offered   to "forge" the rest of her
                      name, as a joke

but don't.

              #

          The nice lady
            lets us
                  have our money.

(Pay Day at the EAF.)

Tim,
        in WA somewhere, is writing his journal poem

as I am too maybe
                    tho if this suddenly *shapes up,*
ends
        on some interesting note
                       —artfully fluffed,
                          but 'final'—
(like the free-form gymnasts at the Olympics,
        that last move, nearly always, fudged)

Well
I'll be watching.

(Meanwhile: journal journal journal…)

I wonder what the multitude is up to now,
                              Tony Negri?
Maybe they're texting.

                    'Bashir'—the name
of the guy serving coffee

                    he offers —

                    so I tell him my own.

                              #

                    An exchange

                              #

As he's thoroughly Australian
                              tho part, probably,
of a migrant family
                    (his beautiful sister is here this
                                        morning),
(looking at her nails, texting)
                    my name won't seem
terribly exotic.
                              Scottish?

Will he figure me as Anglo, protestant,

                      'old' Australian?

I forget I *am* an old Australian,

              in the other sense.

He'll see me as "that old guy"

                Where am I going with
                    this?

2

Dark Heart

Tale of Two Cities

I wonder if Pete is at Self Preservation—his coffee shop—
much, these days? He is, I guess, if it still does the job

—or will it have 'ceased to confer change, respite', become
the wallpaper the ceiling you have, in his words "stared

too much at"? I like to think of Pete there.
I imagine clatter, his awareness of what goes on.

Am I so aware?
Not really.

The coffee here "is good"—tho not as good as Peter's.

I should probably just 'Ask For It Stronger'.
Will I?

I'm glad I thought of reading him again, & came
to this solution—'faced it' even as a problem. Self preservation.

A small problem—but since I solve no other ...

Where Pete sits—just inside near the door—on the black
divan or bench, *I* sit similarly, at the first table.

#

Tho in Adelaide   —   to his Melbourne

#

Aside from the two girls who serve,
there is not much going for it—I look at the street

because the interior is not sufficient, the customers not usually
                                                    interesting,
to me.

                        #

                                There's
'*nothing else*', between here & work (the street
in a long despond).

                        The length of the *walk*
recommends it.

Even so, you *get* here: & then it's not enough.
I will abandon my coffee shop. When did I

last do that? Usually they fold, & *then* I make a choice.
I could move 'next door' (two doors down). Actually,

                        #

I don't like the street. (I could move: 'to a new side of town'.
As in the song.)

                        #

This is momentous. What was it
Lenin said — "What is to be done"?

                        #

What was that song Lenin sang?

When he sang that song —
what did he sing?

The two Korean women who serve here are very nice

An even further walk is the *Boulevarde*. I could go there—
forget the coffee!—& be in touch with *life*—a fugitive

from my class & kind, *a spy in the house of*
nuts,

whom I have known—
to nod to now, various of them, for decades

some acknowledge me, some don't—thinking, in all likelihood,
Who is *that nutter?* Or maybe they've just *cut their losses.* They see

a refugee, from his own class—who might
'repair there again'—at any time—a man

with no loyalties

a completely deracinated dreamer—compass marked
Ted Berrigan, Lou Reed, Karl Marx—(& some principles, probably,
      of my father's,

or Theodor Adorno—who *never met my dad*
whom

like the old guys at the *Boulevarde*
he'd have got on better with than me

that is, better with my father—no-one
gets along with them at the *Boulevarde*

#

This is the sudden withdrawal
Of All Good Will   …   for a realpolitik

of tooth & nail? What a day!)

#

did I mean, anyway, "déclassé"? (i.e.,
not "deracinated"?)

#

he *might* have got on with my father better than I did

And what of Lou, Ted, Karl? Can Imaginary Friends
'turn'?

Where does that leave me?
The two Korean women.

#

They know my name—& I know theirs. They have never been
unkind to me. As far as I can tell.

I have never been mean to them.
Tho of course, *I am thinking of leaving.*

#

There are my *real* friends—Michael & Julie, but they are real,
& I am fooling.

#

I read some of the new stuff the groovier press put out—
groovier, but not that groovy—play Lou Reed—& cheer up

I am back on my feet again.
My mental feet.

#

**Romans cultivated the feet
& used its leaves as a vegetable**

the beet, the beet.

#

I will not read *that* poet again. "(M)y surging blood,
my reasoning mind". I read Ted. (I read "*again*, instead, Ted"!

My position being
So much for lyricism)

Some people prefer the internal monologue

And a crazyman taking hostages & shooting them
in the name of an idea, walks free, months after killing his wife

If our laws protected women—
as they protect men, from, say, king-hitting each other—

she might be alive. Along with the others. A patriarchal,
woman-fearing nation. Our is, theirs is. Here, Sydney, Adelaide—

Melbourne, Baghdad.

Ideas are to agree with, disagree with, assent to or discount.
If I hold a dumb one

it is my right—& the duty of others to point it out.

Respect others' ideas?—I respect their right to *hold* them.
But a dumb idea is a dumb idea. I mean,

"just quietly".

'Learn to duck'?

#

Can it really be religion? Not impatience with Imperialism,
the long durée of Western hegemony, Western disdain?

That is, economics & nationalism? But the world is strange—
evidently, & stranger than I had imagined.

I don't have a good feeling about it.

"There are problems in these times,
  But—woo-woo—none of them are mine!"

Lou, Lou, would that it were so.

(Clocking On) Two Cities Two

do you sit
in your regular cafe,
perhaps thinking about
a favourite Wayne Shorter composition,
ordering scrambled eggs on toast,

… the shape and detail
of the light green sugar bowl
has caught your attention
— Peter Bakowski

"Hi Pete,"
—saying that, I feel like I'm

Clocking-On

like a character in *Dark Star*

Recording something

for the space ship's log
& posterity
— or someone,
somewhere,
who may be imaginary
hypothetical.

But "Hi".

And the coffee?
"the price of a
place to sit"
& I read or write here

& it's somewhere to walk to
                              in the early afternoon
a break from work, the desk.

                                        A
slow morning, this morning
                              I read
                         some Stendhal
(an 'Italian' story)
                    played
                              Miles — *'live in Berlin'*
(featuring, yes, Wayne Shorter

so you're right there,
                         Wayne figures).

                         #

                    Coffee.
                                   (Unless I'm
hypoglycaemic
                    I don't order food.)

                         #

                                        I seem
to have been emailing people *all day*
                                   trying to organise
readings, events, launches
                         for the EAF's
beginning year
                    that is, 2015 : back a week
after the Xmas closed period.

And there are other
                                    communications
to make
            —my own—
                        that I think about

an email to Pam

                one to Laurie (about gel, &
                                        Zone magazine
Question: do they ever answer email? — maybe he knows)

reading about Gordon Bennett
                        who died a little while back

his art, that I felt ambivalent about
                                maybe the best *way*
            for a critic to feel
from an artist's point of view.

It was never designed   to make anyone feel *good*

                                But some of it
was terrific
                & hard to forget
                                Very 'final'
stately, classical, forthright
                        objective

                                        God,

race relations!

Will we ever get past it,

                            & actually

live amongst each other?

                  "Stately"

                        the most convincing
                                 word

in the Terry Smith article

                   I was grateful to him for it.

Stately,

          factual, unarguable.

                #

                And I 'go'.

            (lunch, coffee, a walk)

                     #

                            What is

that tune I'm whistling

            Coltrane, I think

'Blues For Elvin'?

         I'll check.

                (Something else

I almost never do.

          'Shifting Down'

               maybe

(check on things)

I go
to lunch,

                    that is,
                              — I'm here   but I'm
not looking at the sugar bowl, Pete—

                                        distant from my emotions
—where does that come from?—
                                        tired a little

bleached,
            bled,
                        spare,
                                    an afternoon
                                            to finish—

by pushing on.

                        This poem, meanwhile, coming—

factual, unarguable, stately?
                              No,

but clocked-on, seeing out the shift

                        I seem to have booked
not DJ Spooky, but someone else
                              with a similar
                                        name

who says *he'll come sure enough*

        but he's not the Spook

I email my boss, whose idea this is

        —to get a current
        email for the guy—

        #

"DJ SPOOKY AT THE EAF"

        is a 'when-worlds-collide'
        sort of event

        #

—but so far these worlds are sliding past each other—

& a comet—from way out there—

        might easily arrive

the *faux* Spooky

        (is this the 'space' theme?

        come

back, again

        'stately accurate factual'?

('Adequate'? is it? as an expression—of the end of the week?

of hypoglycaemia?)

        the Gordon Bennett white figure
ghostly 'soul' of the dead,

        that emanates

weak, troubled, enigmatic

                                (another trio of adjectives

— ghost riders, who appear together   on the horizon —

                                                signalling

trouble or, at least, a *development* in the offing)

                        #

insert theme music here

                        #

                                — now that, I think,
is Steven Kelen. Hullo, Steve—

"Stately" only applies to a few—
                                        the less sensational ones

but less resistible for seeming, at first, muted

(& then it becomes clear what they state)

Leigh Street

Just a changing of the guard?

An English guy goes past
I know his face
alert & quickly inquisitive

pushing a pram
with baby inside. Shorts—(orange)—
& dark T-shirt,

agreeable, & impersonal the way
some of the English are—why not?
why give the world your soul?

Gabe knew London shopkeepers
from whom he bought every day.
They preferred not to speak—

take the money hand over the product.

Adolphe Menjou! how many times
will I see
that face again?

This is a small, compact, chunky Adolphe
bulging muscles
striped T-shirt

(*not,* therefore, like Menjou)
but that great weary wise intelligent
face

Jack Benny joked, when he
made the best-dressed list—
he'd been right
to buy up all Adolphe Menjou's old clothes

Ah—the past, you funny thing
funny sad

he reminds me of a book rep
—Royden—
whom I see every few years,

from the US
Hawaiian
smart

Here in the waffle shop
with Gina
Ally

The dance academy nearby means
pretty girls

The young men all look like figures
from comic-opera,
Gilbert & Sullivan, the

beards,
the steam-punk Edwardian moustachios,
they appear in the street, in crowd scenes

like paper cut-outs

two-dimensional
not quite present

not that I *look like much*

'Adolphe Menjou' is on the phone
sounds happy,
strong, busy—

& accommodating—shucks!
I'd be his friend, ha-ha!

The Mothers Union Centre & Bookshop
how good there is one! The
rest of the street going gangbusters

in an attempt to look like Melbourne—

coffee coffee coffee & boutiques,
& great clothes—
on the many walking by

A high-tech place dealing in 'well-being'
Bowen Therapy & the rest
Kinesiology! what are these things?

Wetly,
it's called *Aspects of Healing,*
'why not I guess'?

& the factions?

The street's
bustle & prosperity
mask it, but the divisions,

the factions, must
underlie, can be
marked as people pass—

'student',
'business-person', 'poor',
'immigrant'

(Asian
& otherwise. Not a lot of
Sudanese

bothering with Leigh Street)

there's a division
of young, & old (or
old-*er)*—

of people *who've got*
tickets on the future, & those

who've placed no bets
who've done their money way back

—a contrast of visibility
& in-visibility

("I wasn't cast
to *be* on this street")—

Many of the girls
are retro-stylish. The guys:
trainers-&-sports gear,

suits
tight jeans,

(the 'young middle-aged'
wears, typically, suit pants
—*or* jeans—
with a shirt hanging out

or, ambitiously,
I see one guy go past,

in black with a very bright tie)

    (not my favourite idea: to look like
    a graphic—
    a crap trump card

    "I've made an effort:

Look at my black shirt, my
purple tie—my very
short hair!")

Outside the Mothers Union Centre—
Or is it
outside the wellness place?—

six women confer,
wearing colourful Islamic costume:
two Indian women dark-skinned &

colourfully dressed (not the saffron,
purple, yellow & pink, of India—

but deep reds, & yellow, gold
& ochre)—with four,
in more placidly cream-coloured apparel, who are

South East Asian—larger,
less intense.
They're doing something together—

but with a different vibe they must feel too:
not the street's agenda
six women:

the Wellness Centre is just too air-conditioned
temperature-controlled, airbrushed, antiseptic

(like an illustration in an optometrist's)—

they must be with the Union—
or with something else all together,
not 'of' the street: the street is retail

& food:

you look busy or you look adrift:
working
or consuming

These women have another purpose

Two Leigh Streets operate
each invisible
to the other

the new
performs its identity as
hip & functioning:

to sell a view of the world
as of its having 'arrived'
If you've arrived too, *that's okay*

(If I concentrate
on the two elderly women
standing, talking, or the ordinary guy

walking
past the waiters-&-coffee crowd,
they look like background

unreal
painted scenery.

focus on the hip
& the ordinary are filtered out—
invisible, irrelevant anyway

But both are using the space together
—worlds that *don't* collide—

The two women have silver hair
one wearing a purple suit
holding a black bag with chain handle

the other dressed in white frock
& cardigan top.
Old friends. Old Leigh Street—

come to see what the new one's about.

I am here, I feel, incognito.)

Dark Heart

I look in here—this
notebook—& see
the notes for the
last review I did,
& note—that I am
about to write another.
Tho I would rather
write something else.
I whistle bop a bit
try not to think
of the vast tide of crap
the exhibition represents,
check the sky: sere,
grey, pale up one end
of the street,
almost Neapolitan
at the other
(pale, but a distinct
blue, some
dark smudged stain
drifting over it,
much closer *to*
than the far blue
behind—blown,
in those paintings,
from a volcano
somewhere at hand,

almost like flak
in the old movies.

         Goya's
mantilla, & parasol—
& the rumour,
nothing lasts)

       #

It makes the
sky darker too
an atmosphere
not a backdrop

       #

a small figure
further down
Hindley Street
is crossing the road—
I recognize the coat
as much as the figure—
but who?

       #

It is about time
I had a drink with Crab.

About time for a
lot of things.

What to do
about this art?

I whistle
'You're My Thrill'
the beginning
—but, whistling it,
I end up,
as always, with
the 'Perry Mason Theme'
(I *think*)
          (it is
so long since I
heard it)

Instantly recognisable
when I was a kid.

I thought I
didn't like it—

now it seems I do
or something
cousin to it.
'You're My Thrill'.

Then
'Couldn't It Be You'—

I wonder
what the
connection is —

the key, the pattern,
somehow relates?

Its calming effect
when whistled.

                    So,
resignation,
'getting on
with things'.
Hate to turn
a beautiful tune
into a tic, a
neurotic response
tho again, luckily,
it is only the
first few bars
I remember
this way,

the rest of the song
is safe,
unretrievable.

When I play it
I smile.

This art then,
what to do about it?
Inflated in scale,
naive, 'done' when
its theme is recognised
— like logos
for a moral
position.
As if the viewer

should tick a box
in approval
& move on
perhaps 'liking' it
on their Facebook page.
(their 'mental' Facebook page)

Does anybody
do that,
like it that much
that they could bother
to register this vote (?)
their
'shared concern'?

I doubt it.

But then
I am whistling the
wrong tune.

I read in Denton Welch
(the *Journals*)

of some gypsies he hears
coming home from the pub
singing 'Bye Bye Blackbird'
1946
My father used
to sing that song.
I love it.
            The
opening notes

of the John
Coltrane version.
                    My father
sang it often enough
for me to know the words.

Denton, near the end—

"Chopin pours over me from the wireless.
 Nothing but this small picture will be left
 of the day. Many years after, people may
 be able to read then say, 'He was cold; he
 watched the sunset; he ate a chocolate,' but
 nothing more will be left to them."

Today I worried happily,
wrote stuff, 'asseverated',
was alive.
                    It was supposed
to get cold—but it didn't.

Hard Pressed

We do a good job, Fulvia & I
for the students,

a large group whose flustered teachers
ask us to
        'say a few words'

      #

we bat back & forth, introduce
the current show—its glamour
its sad feeling for the world etc

      #

then I'm out :   pause,
             at the lights
in the sun,
& walk, on the sunny side,
up the street
       taking in the heat
after the cool of the air-conditioning, the gallery —

             a
fourteen-year old
         skateboards past
in noble wise
      a boy   a girl following
more diffidently

         but still with confidence
the town lively today
              what with
all the art
        tho yesterday a guy died
'under a garbage truck': Gini witnessed it
an old man, she said—
on her way to the coffee shop where she works.
She was upset & had
to tell me.
           I think she had not
spoken to anyone
& needed to talk.
            I read, again,
Laurie's thing from the 80s: funny
& doomy & teenage like a graphic novel.
The young protagonist
                 —down, alone,
beset by a problem or problems,
                     isolated.
His a joke version of himself—
the unhappy unrecognised author
bitter at his reception: when,
when will fame, a "just appreciation",
follow?
        His objections
to the work of others—dark
asseverations—are funny—
& amusing because intelligent.
                (I suppose
it was always possible those things
would never follow.
          Why did I think

the future would take care of itself?
Actually my own situation then
was exactly his … tho I wasn't so much
funny about it—as depressed.
And now I ain't.

                Tho I'm approaching
that age…

        where…   but not yet.

Gini's not here today—it's Ally.
I feel the urge to be kind, solicitous, anyway—
because I was here yesterday—

                but it's
not needed.
Solicitous a day late.

        Something like the 80s—
no, exactly *un*like that, somehow the
opposite, but symmetrical 'to it', 'with it'—
when Laurie was cranky but *I* didn't notice,
being depressed myself (& trying, mostly,
to ignore that).

        I remember it now as
peaking one afternoon:

           a year or two
of gloom now distilled & fixed in an image.

           I picture me
walking across the small parking area
of the nearby pub—almost a sob
escaping from me but suppressed.
I had been writing a skinny, ineffectual poem
about a lost Titian painting, a martyrdom
of St Peter—not the usual St Peter, another one—
'*The Death of Peter Martyr*'—(or maybe

"The death of Peter, martyr")
& considering an ironic identification,
with the stricken figure, its
death-by-lightning,

                        alone in an Italianate landscape
nature 'looking on',

                  wild but benign enough.
Pity poor Peter Martyr, pity poor Ken.
About mid afternoon, time passing slowly.
The traffic thundering, no doubt, nearby.
I wonder when this would have been. '84,
more or less? Later?

                I'm in a sunny mood now,
this day—tho a little subdued, thinking of Gini—
(who's not on today)—'aware'
of Ally, tho to no purpose.
Aware of Laurie:
I think I thought then things were
going well for him—

                  tho not as fast
as he'd desired:

                part of my 'belief'
in a future … that I could envisage
might not look after me, or did for a while,
& after a while it did.

             History.
The Peter Martyr poem should stay buried,
but Laurie's thing is good—

                A Journal of

The Plague Year. So, subdued
I walk back to work—from lunch—
a coffee, a bit of a read—in my pocket
the criticism of Wystan Curnow.

(Spot Check)

"Too many
... of the people I know about,
care about
       are dying"
              a
feeling
      more than a thought

           books of
last works,
      books of late recognition

Jane Freilicher, Peter Campbell
             no one
I know personally
       —still,

I feel like an insect on a twig
floating down stream.

I check Slaven & Leadbitter: who's
playing the piano
        on these Nighthawk
           recordings?

(Bob Call)

      read Gig's article
            on

Vicki V
                    Nighthawk playing quietly
in the background
                    a CD

                              look at a map of Rome

gauging the parts I never went to

parts that join up as, at the time, I never knew
they did

a detective novel, *The Fatal Touch*, has
me doing this
                         read Augie again

on Lee Harwood
                         — his *Collected*
on sale at work —
                         I should let the punters
have a go
                    but then it's mine
                                        or I
order another one

                    the guy who wrote Eternity
                                   on Sydney
                                        footpaths
when I was a kid
                         the shock they gave
of quiet wistfulness
                         & admonition,

                                    & that they
made the day seem more vivid
                              historical,
registered for a moment
                          in its meanness
its noise & beauty

                    the innocence of another
                                era

(the guy who used to wheel the coffin about

—'out of Gogol'—
)
                        (the guy
with the Mexican hat   & (toy) horse around
                                his middle

—beaten up, they say
                    by the police
)

I screenprinted that word
                        "Eternity"
in gold leaf for its appearance in
                          Laurie's poem

"Psychiatry is an evil & must be banned"

That guy.
                    (Beaten up, they say,
by the police   )

Actually, *I*
have never been beaten up by the police—

& may not be, now, …

I suppose that is a hope

Probably a certainty.

Read Adorno again?

Sloterdijk?

Too smart for me,

but sometimes very funny.

The moon is rising

Crying won't help you

Actually,
the moon is long risen.

Cath & I
looked at it earlier, high, surrounded by
mist

a soft, dissolving look
a ball or shield
We check the house

Anna is interested in

       Take it easy, baby

Maggie Campbell

      The moon is rising, again.

   Nighthawk Boogie

          He played
at Muddy Waters' first wedding

        I was there
naturally.

     And I knew Vicki,
a little
    a share house with her
       "The beautiful
trembling Irene
    is taking another pill"

Gig quotes her.

   And again

where Vicki has the city
     "roaring
& sledging its iron name into the ground"

      Actually (!)
'At East Balmain' is a terrific poem
       more real
than anything I will ever write

                  I listen
to Robert Nighthawk again

                  Nighthawk Boogie

Polski Ogorki (An Historical Dog)

Otto von Bismarck   "(T)he tired colossus"

                              (I see I have made
a beginning here before
                    a lone quote
adorns the first page)

                    #

                              I start out
in the crisp cool air
                    launch in,   to
'We're Having A Party',
                         as I pedal into
William Street

                    gripped
                         by a sense of loss

                              I sang it for her
many times
                    late at night
as she trotted ahead   or beside   or lagged behind

                    #

                    songs I sang for Pola

                    #

Sad Mood
You Send Me
You Look Good To Me

There Is Something On Your Mind

I Didn't Know   (Howlin' Wolf)
I Want to Know   (Magic Sam)

Sweet Sue

Don't Worry About Me   (Lyn Hope)
Honest I Do

           #

many more

                      #

              Vale, my little poltergeist

                          my little poindexter

                          "my little Montegolfino,
                          my little Montgolfier
                          my little girl
                          my little darling dog"

A handsome, blue-eyed
husky

I get to work, check the mail on the way.

TLS

London Review of Books

go & read Barbara Pym

for a while

over coffee

that Gini makes, always with a perfect

heart

\#

'You Done Lost Your Good Thing Now'

((B.B. King dies, too))

\#

"Must have been the rising wind rose,

rose up & taken my baby away"

'Welfare Store'

I wonder if she liked any of these?

or thought it was just me banging on?

The Sam Cooke

used to calm her down

just as they do
grandchild Noah

\#

A thought—
DID ROBERT HARRIS RESEMBLE BISMARCK?

#

I probably don't remember either
                                        well enough

I met Robert a few times
                                    Tho not the Iron
                                            Duke

                                    the 'iron duke'
                                    was before my time

#

I remember Robert's moustache

                                    ageing him—

probably as he desired

#

Poem, Ending with a line by Ron Padgett

I bought The Collected
Ron Padgett & as I did so
thought, This book
is about as fat as
as the Ron Padgett section
of my shelf—I
have all these poems,

I even like them best
in their different colours
& typefaces—but no,
at the end of the book
are ninety pages of
un-collected poems
'uncollected'!—worth
it.
One I find amusing ends, *busily,*
"I have work to do"!

                                    & so do I.

                        #

Cath & I watch a serial killer series
                        on TV

Serial killers are inherently a little
                                    repetitive
                        & this guy
— always shown as
            'abstracted' —
                        is extremely boring

very concentrated on his methodical, silent
                                    preoccupation

tho Gillian Anderson is good to watch
                        & some of the other actors — the

        child star, the cops, the women

                              maybe Gillian
is too mannered
                         but that's the story
& the direction   ((she, too, is 'fixated'
                                   etc))

                    #

Alec Blume, Roman detective
                         that's what I want to
                                     watch

                #

I wonder if Bismarck walked *his* dog,
                              thru
the streets of Berlin
                         Of course it would have been
embarrassing
                    was the dog old,
                                   big-&-old, like him?

or a little one?   Either way,
                         'with all Berlin
                                watching'

                #

At home we both read a bit,
                         then I read Cath
some Padgett poems

some are quite terrific—
enforcing unity & sequence
upon parts that are disparate
& it works—Ron, you have
done it again! Like an
avant-garde,

> knowing Magoo

> > I remember being amazed
On First Reading 'Arrive By Pullman'
ha ha ha
> Jimmy Forrest is playing
'All The Things You Are'
> > or he is
if this CD I burned has accurately noted
what track in what order, it has
my favourite drawing on the cover

glass   ash tray   flower   cigarette

black on orange paper

I read some O'Hara, but not to the usual effect

> > > Or is

this the effect?

> Miles is playing too
on these recordings,
> > Live at the Barrel, 1952

quite some time ago

I was three at the time

hardly in to Miles Davis

I remember the yard

a bear I used to set up, to take a dive as I
came past. I would throw a stone I suppose—
as I came, on imaginary horseback,
down the side of the house—& he would tumble
in his hat & black vest   gratifyingly slowly
from the porch

my parents were not happy

so I suppose I wasn't
tho I don't remember

I must have been 5 or 6 or 8? At what age
do you play these games?

Had I seen *Shane* ?
—no, no TV—

was the bear
Lee Van Cleef?   No, no TV

he was old & beaten, more like
Chill Wills or Walter Brennan …

or Andy Devine!

all of whom have died

                along with my parents

                        & you, Pol

What a life!

            Laforgue was there when
Bismarck was
        & hated Berlin
                for reasons we can
                      both
credit
      & understand
              It was a raw, new,
                'frontier' town

with little history

            not as pretty nor as sophisticated
as Paris

        & Germany had triumphed over France

what an insult

        he did not record seeing Bismarck with his
              dog

Many years, this, before the Iron Duke had reached
his 'weary' stage.

                Laforgue affected to be weary

himself—

      with the devotion of *all Berlin* for Bismarck

his every appearance at a palace window remarked

(Bismarck mightn't have liked it much either—

                  or his rival, Metternich)

Laforgue died not too many years after,

                       still young

promising —

      his English wife following him

                both of tuberculosis

Her brother

        was the grandfather, or great grandfather

    of the poet Lee Harwood

          ((himself a friend of Tristan Tzara))

           #

          I met him,

at a pretty awful reading

      (Lee, not T.T.)
      that no doubt he thought

was pretty awful too

      He seemed a nice guy

Laurie introduced us.

(Metternich

was very, very small

        unusually

               so he could not
                 have had

a very big dog

      — how to control it? —

              & one
              very small

might look equally comic

           look at the tiny man, the
              tiny dog!)

(I probably stand midway *between* Metternich & Bismarck

as Laforgue may have

        a pretty average height

But dogless.

      "Dogless, Pol."

Gilbert Place—Café Boulevard

for Lee Harwood

Softly solarized and parallel
two lines echo each other, glow slightly,
in a space that is nowhere

#

                              I am perched
—I 'find myself' so—
                         sitting forward—
                    hand
                         on knee

the knee I've thrown over
                         the leg beneath:

                         I look left,
out the window

                    — of the
                         Boulevard café

(does it call itself that?
                         I don't think so) —

to the brickwork laneway outside—
wet with the rain,

                    that is now stopped

People going past

                    in Hindley Street.

Onto which

                the lane 'gives'

tho who talks like that?

                      Not me

— I'll give you "gives" —

                        but

am I me, right now,

                not, say, Lee Harwood?

                            or

                        someone?

             Anyhow,

a little back in time

                — & looking at the rain, &

thru it,

        at the harbourside road   the *corso*   of Trieste,

                        some-

how

      in Italy

           A land I love   "unreasonably"

'disproportionately'

             ((*conventionally*))

                    but 'love' anyhow

Hullo, *bel paese*,

           kind people,

                              feeling
a little out-of-time,   suspended

                              between a
here & now,
              a then,   &
                         some *near*, near-ish,
                         future

More fragile than I used to be.

                              Wondering
how to explain this to my sister
                         Should I, in fact,
              "explain this to my sister"?

we have not seen each other,
                              have

'hardly' seen each other   since '73

forty years more or less
                              Three or four times
in that interval?

                    #

                    This is the kind of
                         coffee shop,
I will tell Gabe,   where you could still buy
                         a Vienna Coffee,
              I think.   I'll check the
                         menu

as I leave

                    The newish waitress

                                          whom I like

—(who would not know how to serve one,
    she will never have been asked)—

                                          looks

very nice today

                    The boss   gives me
                    the second
                    'free'   —

                    I Must
                    Be a Regular

                                Now I see
or note again
                    what first caught my eye
as I approached the glass,
                                four
                    silver lines
reflected, in the window, on the side that I look
                                          'out':

the metal arms of the café chairs.
                                They catch
the light
            float, disembodied,
                                'upon', or 'above',
the intricate paving without,

                    so that I look thru them
to see
            the wet brick,
                    the grated

metal drains
$\qquad$ that flank at either side, &
a round cover
$\qquad$ removable — like those in Italy, sometimes
still marked with the insignia, the lettering,
$\qquad\qquad\qquad\qquad$ that proclaimed
'ancient Rome', 'Roman'
$\qquad\qquad\qquad$ 'SPQR'?
$\qquad\qquad\qquad\qquad\qquad$ — that might be, by now,
some of them,
$\qquad\qquad$ quite old: early twentieth century.

Ours stem probably
$\qquad\qquad\qquad$ from the seventies or the eighties.

$\qquad\qquad$ People walking past, in black,
black & red,
$\qquad\qquad$ greys,
$\qquad\qquad\qquad$ but black mostly — for winter.
$\qquad\qquad\qquad\qquad\qquad\qquad$ Me,
too.
$\qquad$ Two people across Hindley laugh

as they help each other re-pack rubbish
$\qquad\qquad\qquad\qquad$ spilled from a split bag

a woman, a man
$\qquad\qquad\qquad$ I guess they work in *Burp*
the awfully named
$\qquad\qquad\qquad$ 'eatery' (or 'food outlet'
$\qquad\qquad\qquad\qquad\qquad$ tho
who am I to be so snobbish,
$\qquad\qquad$ make these distinctions?)

                              both, at different times,
stand, hitch up their pants, bend again
                              &
rebundle the refuse

                         A very handsome Asian couple
                                   go past
small,
        smiling,
                    she   in red coat & very high
— 'above-the-knee' —
                    soft black boots
                         soft deeply black suede

                                        Elegant
A kind of gift to the eye —

                              for me, a too old,
not very handsome man.

                    An African girl, eating chips

                                   #

a guy, narrow pants, cap, on a phone.

                                   #

                    Gilbert Place.

                                   #

                              Posters on the wall
for Elton John   *"& his band"*
                              I thought he was
                                             dead
or at least retired
                         & Dylan Moran
                                        A young guy
in clothes too light—homeless I think—
                                   goes past
(I look outside) his
                              figure
large,
       — black t-shirt, black pants, low —

stumps past like a fridge, from side to side

                                   #

                                        A guy,
unintentionally debonair,
                         using a long, furled,
pink umbrella
                 like a walking stick
                                   flamboyant
but not consciously so,
                    lost in thought.

As who isn't?

              — 'Thought'.

                              Each with
our own.

84

What Do I Owe Them?

Should the unique serve to typify?
Have they been ill-used? To what purpose?

Asian Couple

         The Asian couple.
I am inclined to think Chinese—
mostly on the basis of size,
but not Japanese (the man
might be bigger, be
better, less self-effacingly
dressed)—maybe not
mainland Chinese.
She
is a bright shape & colour
Soutine, Sargent, van Dongen—
for the fast, big city.
I like her for her good humour,
appetitive, optimistic—for her
visual eclat. Tourists, or living here?
In the market — for oysters, sights,
real estate?
She has her husband's arm. Both smile.
He is laid back.

African Girl with Chips

The Africans seem increasingly
to fit in. They are a new factor.

Week by week less surprising.
They assert themselves
in small groups, talking animatedly
in pairs, striding, quieter solo.
Perhaps the chips are protection,
compensation, or just a meal. An
ordinary girl—of 18, of 20 or so?
Black jeans, blue top a fashionable
parka, her expression one of
caution, defence, apprehension.
She looks about.

Fast-walking guy

The guy walking fast, phone
pressed to his ear—all for business—
in which case the business looks shifty
tho it may just be his manner—on his way to borrow fifty,
meet a friend, give somebody
a piece of his mind, pick
a car up, have an argument

Homeless

The homeless guy I see him
only from the back, which makes him
more of a 'subject'—'subjects' look out
a window, don't they, like I do—
& think—& as with

those romantic paintings I see
his view—it's mine—he is 6 metres further in—
rounds the corner, moves eastward
with the crowd. Rundle Mall. Somewhere.
Which might be what he is thinking:
where to go, what to do, for
heat, for movement, the long day to fill in.

(The young guy in black—who rounds the corner
of the *Boulevard*—Gilbert Place—thinks what?)

Flamboyant

The thirty-year old with the umbrella,
striding—where the homeless kid
was strictly 'graphic novel'—
has that hipster look,
of operetta.

Debonair. Protected.

*

Each with Their Own

Observations—
episodes in the history
of one's attitudes.

3

Another World

Duty Chart

I remember just before I
go to sleep: I left my bus ticket
in my back pocket—the ticket
I hardly ever use.
I wonder
briefly—
& remember why I have remembered this:
I was trying to think
what I'd done today—
shopped, which I'd done
with Cath (who reads, now,
beside me). And who moves
& turns off her light.
I dug a circle round
the lemon tree prior to
moving it in a week or two, or three,
cleaned up after yesterday's
pruning job on the almond,
cut some wood. An
electrician came—
to approve work some others
had done: 'sign off' on it.
We talked to him. Petted Pola,
had lunch. I ironed
a bit & cooked dinner
a Greek rice-&-eggplant thing
I've been making for thirty years,
read Frederic Raphael's anger on behalf
of Irène Némirovsky (in fact

I've been reading Sebald's books
four of them in quick succession. The
Holocaust "never goes away", as Cath remarks—
you can think, No more! But there is always
another facet, another account
that will claim your attention.) The
day. On my mind—Pam, &
a lot of other friends: I've had to
write about them all just recently.
(I seem to have been 'despatching jobs'
remarkably effectively.) Now I think about them—
a sudden family from the past:
how are they all? Like
children who have moved away,
around the globe, far from home.
I was not their father—*in any way*—
but I remember them all as young
(as they were when I knew them).
(As I was.) Are they
well, prospering? sad? happy?
Pam, tho, I do know. She never drifted.
Pam, are you okay?

Part Two

Another one of those poems where I
end on a question
                          so, effectively, the
whole poem
                    is a kind of feeling towards

its end,
    what it 'has-to-say'.
           Fine
if that is interesting enough, in its
'own right'
    (almost never)
            or if the search
was enough of a journey
         — & tensions,
connections, are resolved by it.
          Best if
I'm surprised myself.
       Indicating
   'Home at last'?
      'Dig here'?
(or *'Go to bed!'*
      the Edith Sitwell quote.
why did I attribute it
      to her?
fun:
   the upper crust name.

       'Home at last'
       means
formal resolution
       Tho not,
Necessarily, much more
      ('Dig here'—
the implication is 'depths'.

        ('Dig
here' means, effectively, nearly always,
         for me,

"down tools!"

       & like unionised
        labour

my mind walks off the job.
      We'll fish another day)

Jenny Bornholdt often seems to have
   'a good talk' with a taxi driver—
  the Wellington taxi drivers being very wise.
The one (page 70) who likes "the sound of the world"
       (because it has 'reason' in it)
       (i.e., rather than radio, music etc)

     There was a time
      when
Taxi! Crab & I would shout. In the pub—whenever
the conversation got too boring.

(The Little Richard song—
      "Taxi, taxi—take me
anywhere"
    on my mind back then.

   Ah, Crab.

Two Melbourne poems, June 2012

In Another Town

I am puzzled,
by emotions
I can't do
anything with.
(Not My Town.)
      Down-
stairs the sound
of the footy Shan
& John watch.
1) Melbourne's
sentiment for art.
2) The reading, that
went so well. And I go
(I will go)
back—
to home
& Adelaide— 3),
with the memory of it.
And 4) Brunswick Street,
Helen & Peter. Ros
& *Kinky Jurlinki*
John & Ann, &
their students—the
poets who will be next,
smart, kind,
sympathetic, to whom
I read, better read
than me—with it

'all before them'
& so whom I love they
look so heroic tho
not, of course, to
themselves Tim,
Duncan, Tina,
Caroline, Sam & Corey
        all of a piece
with the photos of
an earlier avant-garde
                    that
I never cared much
for. But whom I
like—in their
photographs—lean
simply dressed
handsome & plain,
in their shirts &
dresses &
dedication
to possibility &
each other, the
promise they mostly
missed, fell short of

there is something
'glowing' about it
I never assented
to before. Danilla,
Nolan, Hester,
Matchan Skipper.

I see the Whissons
—& like them less,
but I like them;
Vassilieff brings
a tincture of
Europe—that fades,
abandons him: a
life sentimental
for us but
soured for him I
imagine.
            Coffee
& chips, with John,
& we go to the reading
& give it. Life for
us.

Second Poem

Often the
second poem
is the one that
lifts takes off.
That would be good,
as Pam said—
cause that would be
this, this one.
Me, seated,
under a harsh light
in bed—a little
'like' the picture of
Forbes I gave,

Forbes conflated with
the Guston portrait
('self-portrait')—the
late night worrier.
Who?—you say—*Me?*
John?? Philip Guston? All
of us? Yes.
Settling for
very little, happily—
having thought about
Vassilieff—the promise,
mild I guess, that
didn't come off. He brought
some Parisian lightness as
of Bonnard, something
guileless as well that asked
to be accepted, that proved
not enough. Act as if
the world exists, the Surrealists
said. It, certainly, won't act
as if you did &
me, I am barely here.
Tho happy a this moment.

Notes

In Three Parts—loosely connected, these record the day-to-day in the washup from a group exhibition that brought together many old artist- and writer-friends—some I had not seen for quite a while, others I am more regularly in touch with. The exhibition was *'Coalcliff Days'* at the Illawarra Art Gallery, Wollongong, in April 2011. The exhibition was an assertion of the group's presence in the early '80s. John Tranter is a considerable poet, so the rivalrous joking is inevitable, if undeserved. Nicholas Pounder, the premier dealer in rare Australian literary titles, spoke on the night to open the exhibition. The poem's second part is largely addressed to John Jenkins & to our plans for a collection of the collaborative work he & I had done. The third drifts still further away from the Coalcliff show, to my 'present' daily life. All written originally in May 2011—a kind of debriefing.

Tale of Two Cities & *Clocking On*—are both responses to a poem of Peter Bakowski's, in which he describes a daily routine of his in Melbourne— and imagines how it might compare with mine in Adelaide. (At around the same time I began the poem 'Leigh Street'.) The shooting mentioned in 'Clocking On' was the Sydney, Martin Place, Lindt Café siege: hostages were taken & some killed—in mid December 2014.

Leigh Street—a tiny section of Adelaide in the age of high hipsterdom.

Dark Heart—'Dark Heart' was the name of a not very good exhibition at the Art Gallery of South Australia, in 2014, much touted. The relevant version of 'You're My Thrill' is by Pepper Adams.

Hard Pressed—the reader might have met 'Gina' in earlier poems & note that she has become 'Gini'. 'Gini' is correct. 'A Journal of the Plague Years'—the title Laurie Duggan gave his poem.

(Spot Check)—Neil Slaven and Mike Leadbitter—*Blues Records, 1943– 1966, a complete guide to twenty years of recorded blues*: which says that Bob Call and Curtis Jones were on piano; *The Fatal Touch*—a novel by Conor Fitzgerald.

Gilbert Place—written a week or so before Lee Harwood died. The poem partly attempts his manner. At one stage the poem wonders what the *Boulevard* calls itself: in fact it claims "Boulevard café", "restaurant", "Café bar", and "internet café". But no "ristorante" or "boulangerie". The business closed in 2016.

What Do I Owe Them—is a kind of (naively conceived) guilty supplement to the preceding poem. Clearly, observations say as much about the observer as the observed.

Duty Chart—*Part One & Part Two* — a title poem, if anyone could bare a book with 'duty' in the title. The dog Pola features in a number of these poems. I had had to write about friends from the period 1979 to 1982 for an exhibition—*Coalcliff Days*—about our activities at that time.

Two Melbourne Poems—begins with a sense of dislocation that felt odd & inexplicable but worth trying to put a finger on, probably to do with how busy I had been—& how long it had been since I had visited Melbourne. Friends had put me up for the last few days at their place out of town, at bucolic Kangaroo Ground. There was a final reading and, on the way, a visit to Heide Gallery to see work by Ken Whisson, Danilla Vassilieff and photos of the Heide set in their youth.

9 781848 615762